SLICE OF MOON

SLICE OF MOON

POEMS

KIM DOWER

RED HEN PRESS | *Pasadena, CA*

Book design and layout by Aly Owen

Library of Congress Cataloging-in-Publication Data

Dower, Kim.
  Slice of moon : poems / Kim Dower.—1st ed.
    p. cm.
  ISBN 978-1-59709-971-4 (alk. paper)
  I. Title.
  PS3604.O9395S58 2013
  811'.6—dc23
                              2012041555

The Los Angeles County Arts Commission, the National Endowment for the Arts, the City of Pasadena Cultural Affairs Division, Sony Pictures Entertainment, the Los Angeles Department of Cultural Affairs, and the Dwight Stuart Youth Fund partially support Red Hen Press.

First Edition
Published by Red Hen Press
www.redhen.org

ACKNOWLEDGMENTS

I am grateful to the following people for their invaluable and inspiring guidance, support, insight, and wisdom, and for their help in bringing clarity to my work and shaping this collection: Terry Wolverton, Thomas Lux, Erica Jong, the poets at Writers At Work in Los Angeles, the poets at the Palm Beach Poetry Festival, and my Poetry Angel who continues to watch over me. Lastly, I am forever grateful to Kate Gale, Mark E. Cull, and Red Hen Press for believing in these poems and for publishing this collection.

Many thanks to the editors of the following journals and publications in which these poems first appeared: *2011 Poem of the Month Calendar*, Terry Wolverton, editor (Silverton Books, Los Angeles, 2010), "Game Over"; *Barrow Street*, "Bottled Water"; *Eclipse*, "Board and Care Clock"; *Rattle*, "Boob Job," "Why People Really Have Dogs"; and *Two Hawks Quarterly*, "Inertia," "The People in the Health Food Store."

For my mother,
Natalie Scallet Freilich,
June 22, 1923 – November 25, 2011

Table of Contents

I

I love you as certain dark things are to be loved,
in secret, between the shadow and the soul.

—Pablo Neruda

I Lost My Mother at Bloomingdale's

I tell the authorities she just left the store
but you were right there could have stopped her
I was in the dressing room trying on a bathing suit

the salesman fiddling with the straps adjusting them to fit
my top while my mother escaped onto the street
no I.D. money she started walking

up Central Park West trying to find the old nursing home
she put her father back then when I lived so far away
I remember once seeing him in bed blank eyes deck of cards

in his giant chapped hands half-eaten banana by his bedside
smile slowly coming from deep inside when he saw me at the door
like my mother's smile when she sees me enter *her* nursing home

now my mother's searching for her father for clues
about who she is ever was I took her out took a chance had no idea
she'd leave my side the bathing suit was almost perfect what if

they can't find her what if she vanishes into a refurbished brownstone
stairwell her dress on backwards label showing lost forever after
her last outing shopping with me it's what we did what we loved until

Clive Christian No. 1

The cosmetics lady sprays me
with the world's most expensive perfume
as I pull open the heavy glass door
Neiman's, Beverly Hills. I'm here to buy

a gift, she sprays me with notes of plum,
pineapple, white peach—*it'll linger 24 hours
it's what Katy Holmes wore the night
she married Tom Cruise*—now on me,

jasmine tangerine headachy, smelling
like Katy under the covers, imagining
Tom in the bathroom not coming
out. I keep nuzzling my wrist as I browse

through men's scarves falling in love
with myself, wondering if *I* should've worn
Clive Christian No. 1 on *my* wedding night,
not residue of Bain de Soleil left from the day

poolside in Santa Barbara. I'm still searching
for my signature scent: rose oil tinged
with poison, weekend aphrodisiac, forbidden
sweat. I remember how I used to test

my mother's, kept on the blue depressed glass
tray on her dresser. I'd spray up into the air
of her bedroom wave the fragrance onto my face,
think how my friends' mothers were perfume free,

used cold cream, Vaseline, never smelled
more than clean, and on the way out, empty
handed she zaps me again, this time she hits me
with bergamot, lime, Sicilian mandarin, thyme,

it's what Sylvester Stalone wears, she tells me,
it'll linger at least a week, people backing away,
disgusted, as I exit through the main floor:
a woman smelling like a famous man.

Guilty Pleasures

My boyfriend tells me, *put a candy*
on your naked belly, take a picture,
send it to me. I'm far away from L.A.,
Helmsley Park Lane Hotel, silent on the 37th
floor, white curtains opened, picture window
big as a Broadway stage. Lights, not the moon
command the night. I watch them rule,
slowly turn off, as the buildings grow invisible,
disappear into the steel sky. I spot a rooftop way below
bathed in floodlights, two chaise lounges, a table, plants,
but where's the couple that should be making love
in the chilly October air? Why is there so much
candy in hotel rooms all laid out like a concession stand,
right there on the dresser, easy reach, take what you want,
as much as you want, even if you don't want it at all,
not realizing it'll cost you maybe $5.00 for a Snickers,
who knows how much for Kit Kats since they come double,
even if you take a nibble, or just one Skittle, they'll charge you:
open the wrapper, it's yours. Who really even *wants*
candy at night? I'm searching for life inside the blackness of night,
watching stained glass radiate from the top of the Chrysler Building
which appears to be floating in air. At one time, but only for eleven months,
it was the tallest building in New York, until the Empire State Building
took its place. When the Twin Towers were built, it was number three;
when the Towers came down, number two again. *Take a picture.*
I think about that Snickers on the dresser. Not that I really
want it, but because it's there I think I should have it,
because it's so quiet, I think I should keep myself awake.
I lie on the bed, place a chocolate covered almond on my naked belly,
feel the party coming on. *Send it to me.* Suddenly it's in my mouth,
another, wrappers flying, I'm having a dark chocolate fever dream
as American flags below wave the night inside out.

BOTTLED WATER

I go to the corner liquor store
for a bottle of water, middle
of a hectic day, must get out
of the office, stop making decisions,
quit obsessing does my blue skirt clash
with my hot pink flats; should I get
my mother a caregiver or just put her
in a home, and I pull open the glass
refrigerator door, am confronted
by brands—Arrowhead, Glitter Geyser,
Deer Park, spring, summer, winter water,
and clearly the bosses of bottled water:
Real Water and Smart Water—how different
will they taste? If I drink Smart Water
will I raise my IQ but be less authentic?
If I choose Real Water will I no longer
deny the truth, but will I attract confused,
needy people who'll take advantage
of my realness by dumping their problems
on me, and will I be too stupid to help them
sort through their murky dilemmas?
I take no chances, buy them both,
sparkling smart, purified real, drain both bottles,
look around to see is anyone watching?
I'm now brilliantly hydrated.
Both real *and* smart my insides bubble
with compassion and intelligence
as I walk the streets with a new swagger,
knowing the world is mine.

Why People Really Have Dogs

People really have dogs so they can talk to themselves
without feeling crazy. Take me, for example, cooking
scrambled eggs, ranting about this dumb fuck
who sent naked pictures of himself to strange women,
a politician from New York, I read about it in the paper,
start telling my nervous cock-a-poo, blind in one eye,
practically deaf (so I have to talk extra loud), all about it
and he's looking at me, poor thing, like he thinks I'm
the smartest person he's ever heard, and I go on, him
tilting his head, and when he sees me pick up my dish
of eggs he starts panting and wagging his tail, I tell him,
no, they're not for you, but then I break down and give
him some knowing full well that feeding from the table
is rule number one of what you don't do with dogs,
but I do it anyway because he wants them so bad,
because it makes me feel good to give him what he wants,
and I expound more to make sure he's aware of the whole
political scandal, the implications for the democrats,
the hypocrisy, tell him dogs are rarely hypocrites, except
when they pretend to be interested in you when all they want
is your food, take him, for example, right now pretending
to love me so much when all he wants are my eggs, me
talking to him when all I want is to say my opinions with no one
interrupting, feel my voice roll out on a clear Saturday morning,
listen to it echo from the kitchen to the bath, up through the ceiling,
out to the sky, the voice from within, all alone in the morning
as the light from outside catches the edge of the silver mixing bowl
where the remaining, uncooked eggs sit stirred, ready to toss
into the pan, cooked, eaten by whoever pretends to want them.

DOLPHINS SLEEP WITH ONE EYE OPEN

Dolphins sleep with one eye open so they can count fish
that pass in the night, see danger coming, see everything,
all the time, which is why they're smarter than other mammals,

smarter even than humans who sleep with both eyes shut
except for baby Joey, my friend Rita's brother, who always
had one eye open in his crib, staring at his pacifier as if daring

it to move. We'd take turns trying to close his eye, run
if he started to cry and once he never stopped, cried
for hours straight through two back to back episodes

of *Peyton Place* and Rita blamed me though it was she
who made up the game. Dolphins sleep with one eye open
to let half their brain sleep at a time. I understand.

I'd like to put the left side of my brain to sleep and keep
the right side awake for a week, have it stay up night after night,
words floating in couplets, *trampoline whale, jellyfish bandit,*

but I don't want to see danger coming. I don't want to see lights
flicker on the ceiling in the dark, or hear my heart pound
during a dream where faces from my past jump from airplanes,

take me with them, their arms pulling me through the ocean
in heavy boats, *we will get there, we will get there,* the dolphin
keeps us safe, she's watching over us, one eye at a time.

Watching Raintree County at 3am

While her parents sleep on the other side
of her wall, father's snoring, mother's
disappointment seeping through the door

green and purple bedroom, sixth floor,
the girl watches *Raintree County* on her little
black and white, Million Dollar Movie

middle of the night. Thirteen, captivated
by Clift's anguish, Taylor's desire, she inhales
the flickering light, studies Liz as she slinks

inside her hoop skirt, parts her lips just before
the kiss. Next morning at breakfast the girl speaks
with a Southern drawl. On her way to school

she steps over wounded soldiers on Broadway—
her imagined Civil War battlefield—practices
how she'll tell her boyfriend in first period

she's pregnant so he must marry her. That night
she reads Grimm's Fairy Tales to her family
of dolls: *Rapunzel, Rapunzel, let down your hair* . . .

The girl thinks she's ready for what might
climb up, as she loosens her braid and silently
dismantles the lock.

Fever Dreams

As I lower my face onto my pillow
I spot a small circle of dried blood.
Perhaps last night a one second

nose bleed seeped out in my sleep,
or a lost cherry from a midnight
bowl of fruit darkened as it stained.

Maybe my son took an afternoon nap
scratched a bug bite on his head
releasing a pinprick of red.

Could be my husband saw the stain
on his pillow and swapped:
She won't notice, he thought,

*she won't care if she doesn't know
it's there*, but I saw it, still didn't care
even though I needed to know

why it was there.
To go face down into mysterious
blood is an act of courage;

this tiny dark brown spot like doll's
blood, blood from the pillow itself,
worn out from being used night after

night, punched, folded between my legs,
pressed against my dream enraged head,
quietly burning through the night.

My Neighbor's Cigar

The aroma of my neighbor's cigar
drifts through the bathroom window
like a queasy breeze from a gift shop
in Hell. I don't know him,

but he smokes a cigar each evening,
probably thinking about his day,
as he watches the sky go from purple
to black, the color of dolphins turning

in the ocean. I think I'll invite him over
when the psychic comes, the one I've hired
to contact my father on the other side.
We'll clasp hands as my guide stirs

memories that circle the drain of my heart,
like how my father loved a good cigar
but my mother wouldn't let him smoke
in the house. She'd send him out to walk

the dog, and he'd sneak a forbidden Cuban
smuggled in by an acquaintance from 7th Avenue.
When we make contact my neighbor
will light one up as I ask my dad, *how you doing*

in your room with no door, no walls, no ceiling,
no floor? I'll show him a picture of his grandson,
all grown, his dark brown eyes so much like his.
I'll tell him that when I see storm clouds hover

over Griffith Park, I think it's really smoke
from all the cigars he's been puffing after dinner.
I'll ask him where he gets his matches,
where on earth does he flick ashes.

I Hate It When She Says That

I hate it when she says she likes
skinny guys, concave stomachs, long
arms to wrap around her, likes to feel
voluptuous inside their lean hard
chests, likes them to struggle
to hold all of her, likes to feel her
boobs bursting out of their grip,
wants to suffocate them fall down
on them, hear them gasp for air,
shut up, I tell her, I hate it when
you say that, why does that feel
so good, don't you want to feel
protected, safe, don't you want
them to weigh more than you,
don't you like it to hurt, want
their bodies on top crushing you
so you can't breathe, don't you like
to push them off when you've had
enough throw them over to their side
of the bed don't you want to feel a little
scared knowing they could fuck you up
with one punch, don't you get off feeling
their legs pin you down hold you deep into
yourself don't you like knowing
you could lose your breath underneath
their lips . . . no, no she says, I like 'em wiry,
like to get on top and smother them with my
fine self, like to scare them just a little
make 'em worry they can't get up, might

pass out die in the act, I like knowing my kiss
might be their last connection to life, to anything
that moves anything that matters, I always liked
skinny guys since junior high skinny guys I like
them skinny I like to feel their ribs I like
knowing they'll never feel mine and I kiss her
just then just to shut her up I kiss her like
a skinny guy, I can't stand one more word I
truly hate it when she says that.

In the land of freeways, she takes streets

because she doesn't like crossing over
one lane to another, her foot controlling
the gas, gripping the shaky wheel
that wants to veer to the right.
She doesn't like getting where she's going
so fast unsure how she got there or why.
She likes city streets, routes the buses take
or the slow, ratty cars that snake
around corners, wipers on by mistake
scraping soot on their old blades, brakes
screeching in slow motion. She likes getting lost
downtown, an abandoned bridge, street lamps
piercing the fog, overfed crows perched above,
peering down into her car while she sits at a light
that might last til dawn. In the land of freeways,
she takes streets: she may be in a hurry
but doesn't want to die—green signs in her face:
Hollywood 101, Pasadena next four exits,
right lane only, off ramps, on ramps, billboards
for casinos, mountain ranges sneaking up behind her,
a faraway Ferris wheel rolling into a cloud.
She takes streets because she likes to stop
at each light, see a woman pushing a stroller, small
boy's feet sticking out, his big brother lagging behind,
lunch box opened, cheese sandwich stomped
by the crossers. Streets may not take her
to the desert, catch sight of a Jack Rabbit being born,
fully furred, eyes wide open, nor to Big Bear—
seven thousand feet up the mountain—

"meet friendly professionals . . . breathe clean air!"
hold a snow ball in her thick gloved hands,
but streets can take her to the beach—
down the California incline and right up to the sand—
where she can bury her feet and wonder,
who needs freeways? Not her.
She's already at the edge.

SARDINES

We go for Portuguese, my friend and I,
family restaurant by the beach,
nice tables, they bring olives without

us asking, even the bread tastes good.
Do you like sardines? I ask her, *I love
those little chubby ones come in a tin,*

*they're brain food, you know, and great
for your skin.* So we tell the waiter
(nice young guy, accent, wedding ring),

and he delivers us three huge sardines,
not looking like any we've ever seen,
tails like fireplace brushes. We tackle

these shining fish, open them, remove
their delicate spines, fork out the salty
meat, concentrate on each morsel,

careful not to swallow the fragile splinters
like warnings on our tongues, start to talk,
what's new, our boys all grown, spit out

what we don't trust: bones, words, *seen it all,
haven't we? if only we knew then*—a sharp
fragment sliding down my throat—*remember*

our trip to Catalina—*we lost them in the soda
machine room, mine was only three, for God's sake,
we were frantic, hotel people running around,*

walkie talkies—I'm chewing faster, choking
on pieces of fish face, my friend watching,
it's the wholeness of the sardine really turns me

off, she says, pushing her plate as I scoop out
the second eyeball, slip it into my mouth.
It's the *wholeness* that excites me: skin, guts,

brains. I want to taste the murky world
beyond my future, I want to eat what stares at me
in darkness, what has already seen its own death,

and when the waiter asks if we want dessert,
if there will be anything else, I tell him yes:
more eyes, please. I want to eat more eyes.

SHE KEEPS FRUIT LOOPS IN HER POCKET

she keeps Fruit Loops in her pocket
her fingers diving in when she needs

to crunch her spirits lifted by fake flavors
cherry red lemon yellow crumbs stuck

under her nails in the corners of her mouth
tongue streaked green her snack before dawn

her boyfriend found some in bed tells her
this is food three-year-olds crave not her

with boots riding up her thighs how can
she tolerate dried cereal staining her naked

body *I need these foods lay off* she tells him
they are harmless when so much else

can hurt: the way he peeks under her sheets
searching for snacks to crush between his toes

how he plans to empty her box of Lucky Charms
shake it down the kitchen sink

My ears have been numb since Danville,

you say, still shivering, all tucked in your soft blanket,
the one you wrap your legs and feet in, hide them
so no more cold can seep through. Sometimes I've seen you
put sleeping bags on top of blankets, blankets over sleeping
bags, hot tea in thermoses on all sides, soon to be sipped
between steaming breaths. *I get colder than most,*
I've heard you say, you say it a lot: at dinner parties,
to yourself mumbling outside the front door, fumbling
for your key. It's not about living in a warmer climate,
or thicker gloves. Even earmuffs wouldn't matter.
Thin blood? Skinny veins? Not enough hot chocolate in your past?
I don't know. I do know when I feel your ears, late at night
when everyone else is asleep, they feel like frozen cookies—
the ones I pop in the oven and bake for two minutes,
before melting in my mouth.

My Mother Wants Extra Crisp Bacon

I take my mother for a ride.
She needs to get out of the house,
see something green, smell
summer air; she's going
mad. I drive her
through Beverly Hills.
Mom, I say, pointing out
a gigantic tudor, *look at that mansion!*
I say it again because she's deaf.
Now I'm yelling,
LOOK AT THAT MANSION,
she's happy to see the mansion, likes
"all those windows,"
how many people do you think live in there,
she asks me, *do you think they have servants?*
She's getting hungry, wants a BLT.
She'd order those when I was a kid,
always demanding extra crisp bacon,
would complain, send it back,
I'd be embarrassed, protective,
look upset—like why didn't it come crisp
in the first place—why did she have
so many disappointments,
never satisfied by my father's gifts,
that freakish mink wrap, for example, hated it,
he was crushed, you could see it laying
like a dead animal in the road
under the Christmas tree for weeks

covered by dried pine needles.
I touched it once, it was soft, like her cheek
or her arm. She'd cry at the drop of a hat
if you hit the right nerve, which I knew
how to do but never dared.
I take my mother in the car because she can't walk,
needs to get out, see something lively, fresh,
growing, chat with me about houses others live in,
why don't we live there,
always wanting what she never had,
always dragging me along for the ride.

They Only Want Meatloaf

I offered them everything:
coq au vin, skirt steak, lettuce cups
overflowing with pork and mint,

but they wanted none of it.
I offered them all of me:
dancing on a table with scarves,

spread out under a bridge,
water rising inch by inch,
but they wanted none of it.

I offered them a walk around
the ledge of a moonlit sky,
wedged darkness between their toes,

but no, no . . . I gave them one invitation
after another to discover
hidden rooms inside their dreams,

wrestle the echo of their hearts
as the fire burned and we fell asleep,
folded in each other's arms,

but they only want meatloaf—
a meal to sustain them:
the simplest dish I could never provide.

Lips

a poet's lips will kiss you gently
this is not to say the kiss won't be urgent
even wet ending with a sliding smirk
your enemy's lips will swell from a bite
same as yours but unlike yours his lips
will be relieved by the tiny feet of mice
stampeding across him as he sleeps
a stranger's lips will twitch with desire
while watching you across a crowded bus
a baby's lips are ripe with the sweetness
of disaster strong enough to suck off a finger
hypnotizing as a love struck moment
theirs are the lips that never grow old
your grandfather's lips are laced with mint
will move in slow motion you will watch his lips
closely when you are sick or when your pet dies
the lips of the one who loves you will whisper
truth into your ear while the lips of the one *you*
love are the lips you'll grow to fear
your own lips are sometimes cracked
peeled by the teeth hiding behind them

If you like this then you'll like that

If you like smooth bodies of either sex
rolling over you like acrobats from a lost
circus, then you'll like the desert in late

September, miles of tumbleweed clogging
the roads, locked in an embrace with three
strangers as your bags are driven away

by an unknown assailant, your mother's
voice on your phone telling you it wasn't
your fault your father left her for another.

If you like *Daughters of the Moon*
then you'll like Vivian Vande Velde.
If you like summers back east, breezes

flapping over you like warm seagulls,
then you'll like old-fashioned oatmeal
smothered with milk, in a yellow hand-

painted bowl with blue stars. If you like tacos
with extra hot sauce then you'll like wearing
slippers glazed with spikes as you fast walk

the track of your most nightmarish memory,
hands in your pockets stroking the mouse
you save for the good times.

Second Hand Couch

She sees it at an outdoor market
hidden under hats, leopard throw,
straw basket filled with fake fruit.

She's drawn to its rose color,
curved legs carved from dark wood,
imagines resting at the end

of her work day, her mind slowing
like a train pulling into the wrong
station. It smells of perfumed hair

she imagines a woman knitting,
a couple sitting, knees touching, kissing.
She runs her fingernail over a red stain

trapped in the threads, tries to scrape
it away, tosses off the hats, sits down
like it's already hers, like someone's there

beside her. There's a cigarette burn
concealed beneath the pillow. Perhaps
a woman hearing news of her lover's death

opened her mouth, cigarette falling
buried her face in the folds of the cushions.
She wonders what this couch will bring

into her life. What more than the vapor
of a whispered secret shared between
two strangers? What more than her own

dreams on nights too cold or too hot
to remember, perhaps in the arms
of someone she'll inevitably try to forget.

It Lives Inside Him

Her husband comes to her
tells her they must talk.
It's the ballerina on the third floor,

she thinks, or worse he's been
betting on the horses. But no, he says,
something has found its way deep inside

his guts. She laughs, relieved it's just him
being funny, but he tells her it's no joke.
They go to a doctor, find nothing.

You see, she says, it's nothing,
but he says, no, it's something, he can feel it
tug at his lung, crawl from his kidneys

to his spleen, he can feel it struggling—
it's dying inside him.
Every day he takes it for a walk.

He wants to keep it alive until he knows
what it is, wants to confide in it, shoot hoops,
watch old movies, feed it brats and beer.

Each day his wife loads another bullet
into his gun, collects sleeping pills
in her underwear. This thing in his guts

is a third person in their lives,
and she knows there's only room
for two.

II

Her mind lives tidily, apart
From cold and noise and pain,
And bolts the door against her heart,
Out waiting in the rain.

—Dorothy Parker

GAIL EXPLAINS ABOUT MY MOTHER'S GLASSES

Remember, Gail tells me, if your mother
can't find her glasses they may be in the fridge.

She tells me this without judgment, or sadness;
she tells me as if she's reminding me that people

put anything anywhere when they get old, forgetful,
when they no longer care about seeing anything

anywhere. I'm grateful to have this valuable clue:
I've spent hours on my hands, knees searching

under my mother's couch, squeezing my arm
under her burgundy chair, feeling for the metal touch

of her tired eyeglasses. These are different
from the harlequins she wore coming home from work

on the Broadway bus or on Madison Avenue, her heels
getting stuck in the sidewalk cracks, her skirt blowing up

like Marilyn's. These are not the glasses she flung
across the room one morning when I was young

after a hushed phone call; not the ones she left on the side
of the tub covering *The Feminine Mystique*.

These aren't the horn rims she wore to our graduations,
or took off when reading to my son. Good to know

when she calls me in the late afternoon, numb from napping
television blasting, me at work absorbed in other people's

problems, or right before I take my first sip of wine at dinner,
good to know when she calls to tell me her glasses are missing,

that probably a man broke into her place and stole them,
you must come now and see what else he's taken,

I'll know they're in the fridge, icy as the ginger ale that settles
her stomach, stiff as the roast beef, going bad by the day.

BECAUSE SHE CAN'T TELL
HIM SHE LOVES HIM

Because she can't tell him she loves him
she'll nuzzle the wings of an angel, dance
in the pink shoes he'll never see her wear
she'll tell someone else whom she doesn't love
but who wants to hear her say it
Because she can't tell him she loves him
she'll remember she's loved him since the moment
before their first kiss leaning against a wall
sweaty corridor demolished now the shiny
entrance to the Lotus King
because she can't tell him she loves him
she'll roam the field behind the house
where he no longer lives, the house
where no one lives the one she saw
in a movie teenagers rolling
over one another orange tree tall
grass she can hide inside be
the aristocrat of her own dreams
whispering I love you when he leaves
into the sleeves of his coat
so when he puts his arms inside
he'll feel a rush through his body
the wave she'll be riding across his heart

Inseminating the Wolves

Officials are searching for the right wolf
to inseminate Judy and Jasmine,
two sister wolves en route to the L.A. Zoo.
It's harder than they thought to find just
the right wolf for the job. Why don't they
ask Judy and Jasmine whom *they'd* like?
Don't think *they* don't know what's going on.
They've seen the little wolf garter belts
hanging on the bars. Judy and Jasmine talk
when no one's around. Jasmine confides
she wants that wolf in sheep's clothing,
the famous one from the story.
It arouses her that he disguises himself
to trick and eat Little Red Riding Hood
too stupid to know what end is up.
Judy disagrees. He's not the wolf for her.
She wants a real wolf, one who doesn't need
to pretend, or worse, dress up to get his way.
She wants a dude wolf with dead black eyes
who no one would ever confuse with a dog
or a storybook character. The sisters fight
jaw to jaw, growl, bite until they collapse.
In the morning the zookeeper thinks they're dead.
He tells the chosen wolf waiting in the wings
and he begins to howl, yip the most heartbreaking
wolf notes, demands to be let into their den.
The zoo officials escort him in just as
Jasmine and Judy awaken. The wolf thinks

he has brought them back to life.
He thinks that what he has done is even better
than merely inseminating them.
He says his goodbyes, leaves the zoo
a changed wolf, a wolf with no regrets.

CORNED BEEF

When you storm out after a fight
eat corned beef on rye with Russian
dressing & cole slaw, better than going
to a friend's or jumping off the Santa Monica

Pier where the water's too shallow to drown you:
corned beef—salty, chewy, tangy—
life that's rich, without boundaries or fault,
whereas complaining to a friend will exhaust you,

throw you back into vicious fight cycle,
corned beef will relax, soothe you—
sex without dripping or the need to shower—
ponder the reasons why suddenly you get

it's been wrong for years, since the beginning
when you pretended it was okay because of the way
he kissed, held your head back, then the children,
do the Macarena, snacks in baggies, him, you, trips,

relatives, hotel rooms close to the pool, runaway kites,
bloody noses, this was the good life, spitting on his clothes
when he was in the bathroom, pretending it felt good,
crying into your three-year-old's socks, corned beef,

unless too dry, a little Russian dressing,
cup of tea or straight vodka thrown back, like you
on the bed, naked, waiting for the newest assault,
imagining the children grown, gone so you could be gone too,

so next time you storm out after a fight
you won't be back, salty from crying you'll be racing
the moonlight down Santa Monica straight to the pier,
shooting stars, waves eating out the darkness.

SADNESS

Today everything made me sad.
I tried to cheer myself up
but nothing worked.

I reminded myself that I don't have
the debilitating, albeit rare disease
where your muscles turn

into bone. The sixteen-year-old girl
in the UK who has it still went to the prom
even though she was growing a second

skeleton inside her. I can't even go
to the supermarket for milk,
and I have nothing wrong with me

except my left toenail keeps cracking
and they can't figure out why.
I made myself watch a small white dog

bark at its own reflection in the front seat
of a van, thinking that might break the spell,
make me laugh, like watching a mini circus

without the clowns, but I realized I was all alone
pretending to share a moment with a dog
who didn't know me.

I fantasized crashing my car into a pole,
being rushed to the hospital, laid out on a stretcher,
muffled voices whispering orders, veering

in and out of consciousness, but my sadness
wouldn't budge. Then I thought of you
wearing your fabulously silly socks,

and how once when I was a girl I told a joke
at the dinner table and no one laughed,
and though you didn't know me back then,

I know *you* would have laughed, smiling
that smile, you rushing through me
like a song played over and over.

THEY'RE TAKING
CHOCOLATE MILK OFF THE MENU,

and that's only the beginning.
I hear other junk food is at risk:
brownies, pastries, name it,
they're removing it, the only chance
fifth graders have at happiness.
The only thing I looked forward to
was chocolate milk, especially after
getting yelled at by Miss Paniotoo.
I once poured a carton over her "in"
box, watched the ink bleed down
the equation-filled pages, blurring
the names of my classmates,
never told anyone, not even Donna Nagy,
and now they're taking it off the menu.
What will our kids be forced to do?
Will they devour each other?
Eat one another's faces, run across
the handball court sword fighting
with dry straws, wasted with desire?
Word just in they're even removing
strawberry milk. We never had that.
I'm sure it didn't smell like the chocolate:
a little sour like yesterday's dessert.
We had to drink it before it turned,
when it was still cold enough
that even our mittens couldn't protect us.

My Mother Has a Fitful Sleep

My mother has a fitful sleep,
dreams of car rides that never end,
people pushing to evacuate the building,

swans inside of swans, words trying to form
in the shape of giant O's, bunnies shaking
dust off the tips of their ears. My mother

has a fitful sleep, she's in the hospital
can't eat, use a straw, can't hum *Impossible You.*
Her body tries to roll over, damp as a squeegee

after a ride across the windshield of my dad's
old green Ford. She always had earaches on long
trips south, heading from New York to Florida,

me stretched across the back seat reading
To Kill a Mockingbird, parents smoking Camels,
bickering where to eat, she had to pee, he tried

to please, those biscuits in South Carolina,
the red haired waitress at the diner. My mother
has a fitful sleep, hears the groans of the man

she once married, my father, his hands like trout
on a hook, heat hissing off him like the radiator
their towels would dry on in the old apartment.

My mother has a fitful sleep, legs twitching,
she nibbles her arm as if it were buttered toast,
her body releasing mist from the hurricane inside her.

THOSE PEOPLE FROM CLEVELAND

Remember when we couldn't find
the scissors, corkscrew, wire cutters,
silver nitrate we kept in the napkin drawer?

Remember the buckets of roses,
tenderloin steaks dripping with juice,
suitcases left outside our door in the rain

filled with body parts? When they arrived
it was clear they were here to stay
and we had to say yes, first because

of their joyful dispositions, but later
their urgency pulled us closer,
we couldn't separate ourselves from their

middle of the night secrets, confessions
they swatted around the room like flies
at a sticky Ohio picnic, lies that draped us

like flannel sheets we'd kick away in sleep.
Remember when they left so suddenly, how we
missed them, wrote them notes on the backs

of our knees, looked up at the sky, our eyes
shut tight counting backward hoping
to bring them back, our last slow drip of life.

Skin Deep

"My husband's eyebrows are a total mess
and I think it's affecting his career,"
says a quote in the *New York Times*.
It reminds me of the day I was shaken
by a bank teller whose eyebrows
looked like two shag rugs thrown onto
his roomy face and I wondered
would my money be safe handing it over
to a man whose eyebrows looked alive?
It was then I realized grooming could make
a difference—men may choose to ignore
their excessive brows, but really, is that
the right choice? I took this as a cue
to immediately wax *my* entire body,
invited my friends over, male *and* female,
we waxed and tweezed all day, all night,
the man from the bank—he was there, too,
we held him down while we plucked each
wild hair, tamed his brows so he'd no longer
scare people like me. "*A consumer survey found
63 percent of men regularly trim their ears,
noses or eyebrows, 69 percent their groins,
44 percent trim their heads, chest or armpits.*"
Are we destined to become a nation of hairless
souls, sporting just a few unwieldy strands wrapped
across our foreheads like bands of Italian silk?
I am a marble statue shining in the sun, smooth
as a Barbie. The bank teller stores his eyebrows
in the drawer with the cash; takes them home at night:
cushions for his cufflinks. On weekends he gives them
to his daughter to use as mats in the master bath
of her dark and dreamy dollhouse.

iPhone

people tell me get an iPhone, do it,
surf and talk, hear a song, be a part
of what's going on—so i get an iPhone,

apps for cooks, pets, sex with no legs,
read what strangers say about nothing,
and i touch the app for *pioneer living,* suddenly

i'm standing in the wilderness, circa 1872,
wearing a gingham dress, my hair a long
bedraggled mess, my children surround me

carrying buckets of water from our well,
my husband holding a rifle, but my phone
doesn't work, reception sucks in the wild west,

my girls tug at my berry-stained apron—
mom, let's bake—in my real world i didn't bake
but with this app i can, and now i am,

and the apple pie i pull from the oven is better
than any i ever bought at bristol farms,
and we're giddy as we break off pieces of crust

with our soil laced fingers, try to scroll e-mails
from 140 years in the future and i wonder which
is the app for getting us back? for now, iEat, iLove,

iCome, iAbide, iStretch, iBite, iDecide if i'm ready
like a dropped call, to re-connect, find that special icon
to touch, the dimming app to bring us home

What the Wind Did

She hears it in her sleep
Ruining each dream like
The punch line of a bad joke
Sweeping of Santa Anas
Branches flying over the roof
Sparrows driven from their nests
Patio furniture tossed like confetti
Garbage flying like chunky crows
She wakes up to drain pipes moaning
Remembers a night of falling through
Noise, shaken through her dreams
Let's go see, she tells her dog
Let's go look. Let's see
What the wind did

We Have Legs, Too

Each day we climb the mountain:
sometimes in groups, holding hands,
sometimes just couples, or alone
stamping our feet, doing cartwheels,
painting our faces the colors of hell.
We climb one careful step at a time,
feel the earth below our bare feet,
soft clay molding to our soles,
Jagged-edged rocks piercing our toes,
boulders slipping away.
We want to reach the top, know
all we can. We want to know more.
Our pockets stuffed with sand,
chipped shells, bone shavings,
we try to keep pace but we cannot
keep up. Some stumble over others,
piling up like corpses in a discovered grave.
We want to know more. We want
to get to the top so we can look down
on those who haven't made it up.
We can hear their screams:
"We have legs, too! We too
want to know as much as you
so we won't die alone."

DISCOVERIES

There are even discoveries to be made in making
the bed, she thinks, as she pulls one side of the comforter
more to the other side. It never fits just right,
like a tablecloth that's too short for the table,
there's always half an inch of wood that can't be covered.
Which side do you allow to be shorted? His side
or yours? His head of the table, your side of the bed,
the part that drapes over your feet or covers your head?
Someone's always not going to have enough.

Floating in Hot Springs

Hot wind spins the air dry,
white kisses blast my lips,
skin tight against lizard air

as I float naked in hot springs
face a sky baked blue
by emptiness. I like this—

give myself to the steaming
flow, feel the water's pulse
erupt from the earth, stay

all day as my thoughts
burn through my eyes.
I watch a mourning dove

on a branch laced with red
flowers, cooing at the petals
it thinks are berries, hungry

for a taste of what's not there,
life pretending to be life
in another form of life,

the dove refusing to move,
hanging on like I do.
My heart waterlogged,

I pull myself out
from the springs
to see the bird finding

seeds inside a shadow
of the one cloud
brave enough to form.

While Washing the Dinner Dishes

Tonight as I washed the knife
I wondered what it'd be like
to cut my arm off

right below the shoulder, saw back
and forth through tendon,
fibrous tissue, deep

into muscle, red spurting down
onto the hardwood floor,
my dog licking it up,

wondered how that much blood
would smell, how other-worldly
the pain would be,

white screeches inside bone.
I imagined what fine dinner
party conversation it would make,

me with only one arm, *no I can't help*
clear the table, I only have one arm,
I cut the other off after I washed the knife,

and people would be shocked,
demand to know why I did it, what was I
thinking, what happened to the arm

when it hit the ground, and I'd tell them
my dog carried it off in his teeth,
tried to bury it under the tomato plants,

dug for hours, but the soil wouldn't give,
so he flung it over the fence into the crazy
people's yard.

This is what I imagined while washing the knife
at sunset, looking out the window,
watching the summer sky turn

the color of dried blood, color of secrets
my mother once shared years before
I could hear them.

A Table Near the Water

You're pleased I can get us
a table near the water,
Florida, first clear night

after the rain. You slap me
high five like a volleyball
coach after I spike the ball

when no one's looking.
Lights from the boats
slash the bay like neon

swords, cut the deepest
waves with flashes of color:
red, green, stop, go.

This is our secret. We will
never tell, not even each other.
Far from our homes we watch

who might be watching
us, watch as the yachts
cruise under the bridge,

say how much we wish
we were on one, just us
below deck floating south.

Maybe then we could uncover
another layer of the other,
maybe then we could take a dive

into uncertain waters.
We've been traveling the same
path of longing dressed up

for desire, fighting sleep
with the same dream
that keeps us awake.

It's Not That

Every day I tap on the skull
of another dilemma:
which part of my heart

will I extinguish
which thought will I murder
what lie must I tell?

It's not that
you weren't once everything
I thought I wanted

it's just that I'm done
trying to pump milk
out of someone else's soul

get underneath another's body
squeeze their juice
into my parched mouth

It's not that
you haven't given me everything
you had to give

it's not that I didn't take it
a starved cat pouncing
from one shoulder to the other

it's not that
the pebbles in my throat
keep me from swallowing

it's that however near
or far away
I can still hear

you breathe
though I can no longer feel
the beating of your heart

At the Airport

I trust a stranger to watch my bags,
I have to go to the bathroom,
have to, can't wait, bags too heavy

to carry. *Stupid*, you think? Maybe,
but the round woman in red
sandals had a gaze that held my face,

eyes steady as air, fingers threaded
like a teacher's. I wonder would I
have asked her to watch my baby

in his stroller at the park while I ran
to my car? Would she watch my bed
during the day, report to me whose cheek

settles against my pillow while I'm out?
Can she contain my thoughts
as they erupt, put them in order,

allow me to leave them with her
on the floor by her feet? Might she follow me
into my garden, protect what I cannot:

my son as he enters adulthood,
my mother, deteriorating like a tenement?
Could she hold the plane while I fly

let it down as gently as the butterfly
that landed on my shoulder the day
I married when none of this would have

mattered? I ask a stranger at the airport
to watch my bags and now I worry what if
she takes them away? What if she finds

an empty place where they've cancelled
all flights, where no one waits to go
anywhere, what if she ravages my things,

pulls them apart, finds the white slip
so sheer you can see straight through
to my heart? What if she tries it on?

DREAMS DO THAT

What do dreams do, she asks, staring up at him
like he was a cloud about to burst into showers.

What do dreams do, she asks, her fingers
circling his shoulder, smiling the smile she does.

I saw you in my dream last night, she tells him,
you were kissing a girl on a swing, she had no pants

just a sleeveless yellow shirt, white stripes,
she was rocking back and forth, you held her still

with your lips, I was jealous of the kiss, you peered
over her head saw me watching, mouthed a word

I can't recall, faded away in the middle of the night
like the tail of a comet or the end of a song . . .

Dreams do that you said, they fizzle out in darkness
like spent fireworks. Yet, she believes important dreams

sleep in the pockets of our hearts, folded
like handkerchiefs, waiting for a special occasion.

STRANGE LIGHTS NEXT DOOR

She keeps her nails short
So her boyfriend can go home
With his back unmarked

She teases herself
With the idea of scratching
Until his blood flows

An endless stream
Hot red covering her hands
Dripping down his sides

Cementing their bodies
She keeps her nails short
So she can't satisfy her own

Itch waits for him
In darkness candles burning
By her bed flicker in front

Of the shades making pictures
The couple next door watch
In shadow as they argue

About shapes they think
They see or don't see
The man sees only

Strange lights next door
The woman sees hands
Reaching for the moon

How to Shop for a Poet

Before shopping, ask yourself,
what kind of poet am I looking for?
Perhaps you want a clairvoyant

amnesiac poet who'll recite your future
then forget your name, or a handy
poet, who'll mend the holes

you've punched into your walls,
boss you around in couplets:
where's the glitter, where's the chickens,

don't touch the stew until it thickens.
You can find an assortment of poets
in the stationery and picture frame aisle

though you might also try intimate
apparel. Pack a snack in your pocket,
so you can feed your new poet

on the way home. Keep in mind poets like
covered snacks which they can unwrap
slowly, on their own. Be sure to examine

your poet carefully. Pry her mouth open,
look down her throat for what she's about
to say: her job is to tell the truth for as long

as she can, only to crack like a jar of pennies,
roll off the counter, spill across your floor,
her sobs echoing, people wondering *why*

*did he bring that poet home, what
was he thinking?* Prepare a proper spot
for your poet: desk and chair hanging

from the ceiling, open window so she
can dip her toes into the air, trampoline
below. Before shopping ask yourself why

you want a poet at all? Is it the comfort
of rhyme you're after, or is it free verse
you crave: a warrior-poet who'll asphyxiate

you with words, teach you to savor the shadow
that haunts you, explain why thousands
of blackbirds fell from the sky, or why

the elephant in the tree searches for his nest?
You want a poet who'll confess, press you
into consciousness, feed you purple grapes

from her stained silk glove, help you to hear
the silence of your song, leave you saturated
with meaning, already aching for more.

EXTRACTION

My dentist tells me it's the longest root
he's ever seen as he uses all his strength
to pull out my top back molar been hurting
since as long as I can remember feels like he's
extracting my brain forcing every thought
I ever had out of my head longest root he said
my mouth so numb I have no mouth
the tooth doesn't want to leave its warm
dysfunctional socket headquarters from which
it's been tormenting me for years lighthouse of pain
tooth that reminds me everyday that everything's
not okay let me see its calcified pulp let me roll it
in my fingers remember my mother leaving me
alone in the dentist's waiting room reading stories
in *Newsweek* about the soldiers coming home
man on the moon get the tooth out remove
this neon time bomb red alert tooth depleting
my good will let me worship it for showing me
what hurts can be removed will end let me
wear it around my neck to prove even roots
that have fused can be ripped out

III

Dying is a wild night and a new road.

—Emily Dickinson

New Year's Eve Party

Tonight our red dresses hug our bellies,
glitter is in our hair, gift-wrapping paper
sticks to our shoes, our shoes stick
to the floors of other people's kitchens.
Ranch dressing, everything fried, cold air
packing us inside, we gather to say goodbye
to a year that slid under the door like
an unopened utility bill. The party bed stacked
with coats over coats, car keys, weed spilling
out of pockets, tufted comforter covered
with handbags, intermingling scarves, dog hair,
one lost slipper sock, you on top, your hands
on my throat pressing just hard enough for me
to say, *Happy New Year*, lint ghosts trapped beneath
as we drift off into the demanding silence of January.

The Salvation Army Won't Take the Futon

Because it's not a couch, not a bed,
The Salvation Army won't take the futon
from my mother's apartment. It has to be one

or the other, not in between, like my mother,
who's alive, but not really here.
The Salvation Army truck is taking the stuff

she'll no longer need, blue porcelain jar lamp, end
table where she kept my phone number, her tissues,
hard candies, burnt orange velour chair from which

she watched TV, argued with the news, critiqued
Diane Sawyer's wardrobe—*too much beige*.
I'm moving her to a place where ladies' faces break

into smiles for no reason. The movers lug her things
onto their truck, each piece caked with the kind of dust
that settles after we give up. They don't know she's trapped

in a Board & Care, propped up by pillows someone
recently died leaning against. I beg him to let the rules slide.
Who'd ever know it's a futon? The luscious fabric,

the pattern? Who would ever question this wasn't a couch?
My mother just liked the word, that it could be both,
she liked knowing it didn't have to be one or the other.

Hotel Room

fragrant as the inside of a box
of fine cigars, warm, seductive, inviting me
to travel through dreams I've never had:

I'm in a smoky waiting room outside
a magician's office, preparing to be examined
my body wrapped in seaweed

my Chicago hotel room 23rd floor
of the sky, silent as snow falling in a forest
with no trees, I hear nothing inside nothing

the room is large, two full beds, two baths
just for me, I wander from one to the other
I am my own guest

HIS OTHER GIRLFRIEND

"My *other* girlfriend lets me," he says while trying to stick it in
without lube. I don't care what his other girlfriend lets him do
or if she wears red satin dresses that slip off her shoulders,
has golden hair, can recite *The Wasteland* without stumbling,
I will show you fear in a handful of dust, is a landscape architect
who handpicks bricks that separate gravel from vegetables,
designs wagon wheels filled with purple and pink roses,
can drink an entire pitcher of beer in one gulp without burping,
writes in Japanese while humming the theme from *The Third Man.*
"My other girlfriend has her *own* girlfriend," he tells me, "they tip toe
up my back, dive from my head to the couch." Why does he have to
tell me about his *other* girlfriend—me who can recite all the dialogue
from *High Plains Drifter* while walking on my window ledge,
twelve stories high, still believing there are reasons not to cry,
me who wades into the roughest ocean, puts my head below the surf,
swallows mouthfuls of fish that float down my throat, swim out my ass.
I've been cross-country skiing my way into his heart for years,
and the moonlight on the snow is beginning to fade.

Sorry

She's sorry for saying she hates him
though he says it right back,
like they're in the same club, no rules,

skin rolled up, family postcards
yellowing on the fridge. She's sorry
he wants to live in a cave with only

a PlayStation and food. She's sorry
for the hole she shoots through his chest
with her imaginary rifle, smile spreading

across her face. Being sorry is a small part
of what keeps them together. He's like
the faded pink sweater stuffed in the dark part

of her closet: she can't throw it out. It's the one
she wore back then when he slid his hand
into hers, and she froze as her heart

pounded out her future. So what if her nights
are spent picking broken glass from her bare feet.
The earth is still moving for someone.

BOOB JOB

Trying on clothes in the backroom
of Loehmann's, a stranger invites me
to feel her breasts, a stranger trying on
dresses that don't fit and I can see
her breasts are larger than they want
to be, and she can see I'm watching,
asks me to help zip her up and I struggle
to pull her in, smooth out her sunburned skin,
tug, ask her to shake herself in, she tells me
she just got them, didn't know they'd come out
so big isn't sure she likes them, not even her
husband cares, he's not a breast man, she says,
he's an ass man but I'm not getting an ass job,
good, I say, because how do you even *get* an ass job,
do you want to feel them, she asks, and I do, so I do
and they feel like bean bags you'd toss at a clown's face
at a kid's party, I squeeze them both at the same time,
cup my hands underneath them, she says, *go ahead,*
squeeze some more, it's not sexual, aren't they heavy,
I don't want to have them around every day, her nipples
headlights staring into the dressing room mirror, red scars
around their circumferences, angry circles I want to run
my finger around, *you should have seen them before*
I had them lifted, they were long drooping points,
couldn't stand looking at them anymore, can I see yours,
so I show her, so small hers could eat mine alive,
nipples like walnuts, do you think I should make mine
bigger, and there we are examining one another's boobs,
touching, talking about them like they aren't there,

don't matter, forgetting how it felt when we were twelve
or thirteen, one morning when they first appeared
sore, swollen, exciting, new, when they had the power
to turn us into women we no longer knew.

No One Bleeds Forever

for Grace Paley

They sat on the bench—Washington Square Park
Grace and my mother, before I was born
my mother with my older brother,
Grace with her own.
Quirky, my mother told me, years later,
when I asked, she was *so different before*
she wrote her stories, before my mother
would move uptown into her new life.
They had the Bronx in common—the place
no one wants to admit they're from.

Grace would wear *these hats* she'd tell me,
we had so much to talk about the babies those feelings
she was *bossy,* a young female writer 1950
sounds so romantic now, but Grace had to scoop
her children up and give them baths,
just like my mother, had to stick thermometers in them,
feed them green purees from jars, had rough hands
from washing out diapers.
And, like her characters, she had hope, just like my
mother who always believed, *no one bleeds forever.*

Why Do They Do That?

Why does she wear lipstick to bed, he wonders,
as he turns off the overhead, lights a candle, sits up
with a book he'll never finish about a Scottish family
from the 1800s. *Who cares*, she wonders,
why would he read about those dull people
when I'm laying next to him—a fiercely soft,
sword swallowing incubator of heat, a lipstick-in-bed
wisp of woman. Yet, he keeps wondering,
Why does she do that, as he smoothes the sheets
with the soles of his feet, settling his long body
under the covers. *LOOK GREAT IN FOUR WEEKS,*
her magazine promises: she's ready to learn, not
that she doesn't already look great, but, hey,
you can always look greater, then maybe he'd stop
reading about those people, smear that crimson
right off her mouth, the red she wears to bed
because it's slick, tastes like morning, lets her pretend
she's a movie star wanted for murder, a runaway
with a price on her head, her mouth untouched,
harboring a kiss filled with someone else's future.

Little Glass Dishes

Cleaning out my mother's cabinets
I spot them buried behind dusty mugs:
little glass dishes, set of twelve, thin

but hearty, like my grandmother we called
Nana, round, the size of a gigantic pancake,
the size of my grandfather's palm, a thistle

engraved around the side, been in my family
since the Depression, used for stuffed cabbage,
piroshkis, a Chesterfield or two extinguished

in a plump baked apple, shrimp cocktail
in the better years, served to the family, to Hyman,
the boarder Nana took in, found him at the newsstand,

corner 96th and Central Park, liked his lefty politics,
lost his right leg in a war I'd never heard of,
had a wooden one he'd let me and my brother knock

if we were good. Now the dishes belong to me.
I took them when I moved my mother to the home.
There were other things—a garnet ring that never fit,

stack of letters I couldn't get myself to read—
but I wanted those dishes. They reminded me
of holidays when I was a girl, bundled in my camel hair

coat, back seat of my dad's green Ford, on our way
to apartment 3B where me and grandpa would play
gin rummy, chocolate bars stacked high on the cold

windowsill, listen as the dishes got cleared
to make room for the next course. That was many
meals ago. This morning when I scraped the food away,

ran my fingers over the magical glass, I could see
both sides of my hands. I could remember
all of us bumping into one another in that crowded

kitchen, feel the heat from the oven, smell the food
coming out see Nana's small hand shake as she sliced
the noodle kugel, crisp on top but never burnt.

Ninth Grade Boyfriend

Catalina's, Saturday night, Charlie Haden
playing his upright bass, eyes closed, fingers
down there on the strings, precise, sure,

my eyes closed, too, feeling music
with no melody, just pulse, unresolved,
Watts on sax, filling the room with dissonance

like a life well lived, as the memory of his face
comes to me in a wave of fusion.
I've no photo of him, but still recall

the way he smelled of sweat and English Leather.
We'd lie on his bed, top bunk, his finger trying
to work its way inside me, while his little brother

did homework below us, me worrying,
he'll think I'm too easy. I wasn't ready to show him
how to make it feel good, wished so bad I could,

didn't have a clue what would happen so soon
after we'd slow danced with lights out in living rooms
of other parents' apartments, our bodies hanging

onto one another's, our kisses still teaching us,
his cheek smooth like mine, and that next year
when I got the call that he fell off the wall,

Riverside Drive, was no longer alive, I realized
I'd never even met his mother, just his brother,
knew his sister, too, she called to tell me

the news, and tonight, forty years later, in the dark
crowded club alive with music, I mourn his death,
can feel his lips parting.

INERTIA

She sits on her bed all day every day,
wearing nothing but a stained smock

from yesterday's closet. She holds a long
white candle under her chin but never

lights it. She is out of matches.
No evidence of nourishment, she's sustained

by watching clouds hump like the oversized
white cushions plumped behind her motionless

body. A spider twirls its web at the base of the bed,
her tired feet caught in its silken embrace.

She listens to the crows graze their black
taffeta feathers against the dry faded rose's

brittle petals, roses she can't water, hose
she can't lift, garden faucet she can't turn on.

She will, however, brush her teeth twice
every day. Leaves her bed for the bath where

her toothbrush sits straight up in its elegant
highball glass. She does this because she was told

inertia can lead to bleeding gums,
the one thing she cannot abide.

GIVING MYSELF UP

for Mark Strand from whom I stole this

I give up my eyes which refuse to see you as you are.
I give up my ears, false tunnels to my heart.
I give up my heart because a new one is aching to form.
I give up my throat which closes when I try to call your name.
I give up my neck which strains to see the other side.
I give up my breasts, keepers of all your secrets.
I give up my belly, a pillow for those I've loved.
I give up my pussy so I can finally be free.
I give up my ass, the party you most like to crash.
I give up my thighs always hungry for more.
I give up my legs which fight each other in the darkness.
I give up my feet which turned their backs on me years ago.
I give up my clothes, so you can no longer rip them off me,
and I give up the girl who has slipped them over her head
and slipped them back off again. I give up. I give up.
And I will only take everything back when you agree
to join me in the next impossible life.

The People in the Health Food Store

The people in the health food store
don't look healthy which is why they're here.
I'm here to get carrot chips, craving crunch,

flavor, after visiting my mother at the home
where flavor only appears in faint whiffs
of memory, where people in wheelchairs

suspiciously eye the applesauce on their trays
delivered by chubby nurses in red scrubs,
pictures of ponies or baby elephants stitched

onto pockets that contain their syringes and keys
to the lounge. The people in the health food store
look dirty, wear spandex, have spaces between

their teeth, prowl the aisles for natural
supplements, inner peace, ola loa energy drinks,
so only the other losers will die, not them,

not after they cleanse their bodies of all
impurities, destroy lingering negative thoughts:
what if my baby never learns to talk, what if

I suddenly forget how to walk, what if the earth
sucks me deep into hell, like the hell my mother
lives in, where when I visit she asks me,

"who put me here, when did this happen,"
it was only yesterday she sipped martinis
on the rooftops of Manhattan, so it's no wonder I run

for the health food store, fill my basket with Miracle
Cream to rub in every pore, stock up on Wrinkle
Warrior, buy a year's supply of brain enhancers

so when it's *my* turn to stare out the window wearing
floral-patterned daytime pajamas, I'll remember
who I am, who I was, who I once loved.

Board & Care Clock

My mother tells me she needs a clock,
is unsure of the time when she wakes

after a late afternoon nap ever since
she's been in *this place*. I tell her, *look—*

look up there—point to the clock, round,
clear as her grandchildren's faces,

show her the second hand, how it ticks
on the wall above the TV, but she says, *no,*

she doesn't like that clock, wants a smaller,
more intimate clock to sit beside like a friend

in the park. She wants time to be hers alone,
like the chocolates I bring she won't share

with the other ladies in hats who sit politely,
all dying for the same thing: a reason to care

what time it is as the seconds gather like dots
on an Impressionist painting, grey, shadowy

soft edges of intermingling minutes, creating
the illusion of color, light, the culmination of life.

SOLACE

My mother passed away in her sleep last night
after we all had Thanksgiving dinner, and I'm trying
to find solace. When I looked up the word to make sure
I was searching for the right thing, this is what I found.
Seems an awful lot of information to explain a word
that means to console, to make cheerful, or to amuse.
After reading it I thought I might never find solace
because I don't drink whisky, don't smoke cigars,
champagne makes me dizzy. I wondered, too, who
is this man who always bounced back and what *are*
his varied interests? Do I share any of them? I found
a little solace today by eating random foods I'd otherwise
never touch. I had a very rich meat sauce on whole wheat
spaghetti, a glass of red wine, this is not uncommon,
but then gorged myself on chocolate covered dried fruit,
popping them in my mouth, fistfuls of bliss, sips of wine,
then forkfuls of salad, tart dressing, cucumbers, olives,
feta cheese, and it all began to taste the same, just the need
to taste *something* and not remember that I no longer
have a mother I can call or see or worry about.
Where's this solace that so many people are mentioning to me?
Does it exist? Let this stranger have an abundance of whisky.
I'll have my chocolate covered dried fruit and let's see
who'll throw up first. Get him on the phone for me, I yelled to no one.
Let's see how long it took *him* to restore and recreate himself through
intensely active immersion in one or another of his varied interests.
I'll give it a try: a little air hockey tonight, some online black jack,
followed by shrieking an ABBA song at the moon plastered against
the black ice sky. I will find that solace even if I have to scrape

it off the walls with my nails, and I'll bounce back like a handball
off the side of the building where I played after school,
where my mother sat on the stoop with her friends smoking
Kent cigarettes, talking about the war, their sons, marriage, grief,
watched us yelling not to run into the street. I will bounce back
in the same way I surrender to heartache: laying down,
letting the pain of loss wrap itself around me like a lead blanket,
protecting me from the radiation of saying goodbye.

GAME OVER

I squirted too much mustard on my hotdog
and now I can't eat it, I tell my friend at the game.
That's why God made napkins, he tells me—

wipe it off. I tell him I knew God made mustard
but didn't know he also made napkins. I tell him
once the mustard gets soaked up by the bun

it's game over, even napkins won't help.
He's disturbed. I can see in his face he's mad
I wasted a perfectly decent hotdog and worse,

now I'm doubting God. When did you stop
believing in him? he asks me, his face twisted
like the pretzel I'm about to put mustard on.

Did I *ever* believe in God? Was God peeking
through the window, up there in Laurel Canyon
when my son was conceived? Was he in my belly

when they sliced it open so they could lift my baby
out of his warm private ocean? Was God in my son's
hands when he pitched a perfect game at the Pan?

My friend's still talking . . . I was an altar boy,
he continues . . . you don't forget the Eucharist,
wearing the crisp cassock, snuffing out candles

as the priest consecrates bread and wine . . . you
don't forget ringing the bells until someone you love
dies, then it's game over. He tells me these things

our shoulders touching as Manny hits deep
into left field, the men on base run their hearts out,
thousands in the stands praying, *please* God, *please*,

get the run, win the game, as the mustard hardens
on my cold dog, bun stiff, I slip it under my seat
with God's blessing as the first man slides safely to home.

"How was your weekend,"

the lab technician asks me
as she sticks the needle in my vein,
routine physical, blood rushing
up the tube as if being chased
out of my body. *Fine,* I tell her
all good, really good, did some things,
saw some people, ate out, got rid of shoes
I haven't worn in years, craved ice cream,
but had no one to go with, so I went by myself,
embarrassed ordering a mint chip cone
alone in the middle of a Saturday, got over it
when I took a bite, euphoric, no longer caring
that my son was too old to take for ice cream.
Wrote a letter to my dead mother but couldn't
read it at her grave because we cremated her
so I read it sitting at the kitchen table,
a photo of her propped up in front of me.
"Sounds amazing," she says, my blood still flowing
up the tube, new one now as I'd filled up the first.
Where will they send my blood, and how
do they test for all the things they test for,
and what if they discover I have one
of a million diseases one could have, something
to confine me to bed for as many days, weekends
as I have left on this earth, or what if they find
nothing? Will I start to take pictures of my food
like a friend of mine does? He takes pictures
of what he's about to eat so he'll remember
what he put in his body, so if something goes
wrong he'll know it was the yellowtail swimming
in lime sauce or the ginger sorbet with one proud
blackberry perched on top. He keeps files of photos

so he'll never forget what he tasted, what filled him.
I want to taste the blood being drawn from my arm,
wonder if it would taste the same as my mother's.
"What did you do this weekend," she asks
forgetting she already asked. *I had an ice cream cone,*
I tell her, *took a picture of it before it started to melt,*
licked a drop of blood still warm from a new cut,
read a letter to my mother at her grave.

SLICE OF MOON

There's a slice of moon
left over in the sky, a sliver
of carnival glass wedged

into the milky blue,
as if the Gods
had a midnight party,

couldn't finish it all,
left a piece of moon
for us, barely throbbing

in the morning light,
a crescent of white
hanging onto the sober sky.

Why is it still up there
on this new day?
Its job, to taunt darkness,

burn through the night
like heaven's candle,
igniting our dreams,

should be over. Why
does this moon persist?
The sun sets as it's meant to,

leaves the sky gracefully,
falling into the arms
of the ocean.

We can trust it to disappear
so the sky can darken,
so we may rest, rocked

by the pale memory
of motion, rocked by the song
our mothers sang or never sang.

BIOGRAPHICAL NOTE

Kim (Freilich) Dower grew up in New York City and received a BFA in Creative Writing from Emerson College, where she also taught creative writing. Her first collection, *Air Kissing on Mars* was published by Red Hen Press in 2010 and appeared on the Poetry Foundation's Contemporary Best-Sellers list. The book was described by the *Los Angeles Times* as, "sensual and evocative . . . seamlessly combining humor and heartache." Kim teaches in the BA program at Antioch University Los Angeles, and is the owner of a literary publicity company called Kim-from-L.A. Her poems have appeared in *Barrow Street, Eclipse, Ploughshares, Rattle, The Seneca Review,* and *Two Hawks Quarterly.* Two of the poems in *Slice of Moon* were finalists for the *Rattle* Poetry Prize. She lives with her family in West Hollywood, California.